Music  t
Sounds

by Lauris Shaw
illustrated by Kate Ashforth

Harcourt
SCHOOL PUBLISHERS

Printed in China

ISBN 10: 0-15-350437-4
ISBN 13: 978-0-15-350437-2

Ordering Options
ISBN 10: 0-15-350332-7 (Grade 2 Below-Level Collection)
ISBN 13: 978-0-15-350332-0 (Grade 2 Below-Level Collection)
ISBN 10: 0-15-357444-5 (package of 5)
ISBN 13: 978-0-15-357444-3 (package of 5)

4 5 6 7 8 9 10 0940 15 14 13 12 11 10 09

Sounds!

Sounds are everywhere. Some sounds are loud. Some sounds are soft. Music is made of different sounds.

Making music is being creative with sound. Go to a music performance. Concentrate on the different sounds. Listen and see how they are made.

Listen to the Drum

Look at the parade. Listen to the drum. The sound is made by hitting the drum.

You might see some other instruments that you can hit to make a sound.

See if you can hit a drum. Your friends will be relieved when the noise stops!

Listen to the Horn

Look at the music players. Listen to the horn. The sound is made by blowing into it.

Here are some other instruments that you blow into to make a sound.

If you can, try to make a sound on a horn. It is not easy!

Listen to the Guitar

Look at the band. Listen to the guitar. The sound is made by plucking the strings.

You might see some other instruments that you can pluck to make a sound.

See if you can pluck a guitar. Your fingers will need to work hard!

Listen to the Piano

Go to a concert. Listen to the piano. The sound is made by pressing the keys.

You might see some other instruments that have keys you press to make a sound.

See if you can play the piano. Each key plays a different note.

Making Music

There are many ways to make sounds. You can hit a drum. You can blow a horn. You can pluck a guitar. You can press the keys on a piano.

You can give music different
expression by changing the
volume and beat of the sounds.
Music is about sounds.

Think Critically

1. What three things do different sounds give music?

2. Which section of the book tells about instruments you can pluck?

3. What do you have to do to the horn to make the sound?

4. Why do you think the author has used different headings in the book?

5. Which instrument in the book would you like to play? Why?

 Music

Make an Instrument Use materials in your classroom, such as small boxes, cardboard, rubber bands, and string, to make and decorate your own musical instrument.

School-Home Connection Ask each family member what style of music they like the best. Make some music together by using things around the house, such as spoons and cans.

Word Count: 291